OCTOBER 12, 2018

INTRODUCTION TO CYBER SECURITY

The Chartered Institute for IT

U EKPO
MCSA CONSULTING

Table of Contents

Acknowledgement

I praise the Almighty for this opportunity and guidance.

Many thanks to Matthew Ekpo, Neetu Nair and Peter Schonbeck for their support and encouragement.

Overview

Wherever you go, live or work, news on Cyber Security is prominent to the public eye. When asking most people about their knowledge of Cyber Security, a common response relates to the like of 'hackers' or companies that have been in the media as part of a security hacking. In turn, what this can mean, is that quite a large number of people, will be surprised to know that Cyber Security covers quite a large field of activities. It covers technical and non-technical IT activities, legal, forensics, policing, etc. So we could look at Cyber Security as a field which is made up of all the areas where information security has been impacted or has something to offer in making information technology and data secure. There is a simplified diagrammatic representation of the relationships within the field of Cyber Security in the Appendix of chapter 10.

CHAPTER 1: Introduction

Introduction to Cyber Security has been put together for the benefit of those who are new to the field of Information Technology and are interested to learn about Cyber Security as part of a potential career change. This information is to provide the basics about the field of Cyber Security and will also provide additional materials to help anyone interested, improve their knowledge to an advanced level.

Cyber Security is the body of technologies, processes and practices designed to protect networks, computers, programs and data from **attack**, damage or unauthorised access. In a computing context, **security** includes both **cyber or online security** and physical **security** (itgovernance, 2018).

Here are some important overviews;

- **International Organisation for Standards (ISO)/ International Electro-technical Commission (IEC):** This is a joint technical committee. Its purpose is to develop, maintain and promote standards in the fields of information technology (IT) and Information and Communications Technology (ICT).

- **Internet:** This is the collection of the physical devices and communication protocols used to criss-cross the web sites and interact with them.

- **The web:** This is the collection of servers that hold and process web sites we see. The web is not the internet, but it runs on top of the internet, which acts like the bridge for the web. **HTTP** (*i.e. HyperText Transfer Protocol),* is the underlying protocol used by the World Wide Web and this protocol defines how messages are formatted and transmitted, and what actions Web servers and browsers should take in response to various commands)

- **Network:** You have the physical network and the virtual network. This is the integration of computer systems and servers via routers, switches, repeaters, both locally and globally.

Basic components of Cyber Security:

- **Confidentiality:** This is to hide information or resources.

- **Integrity:** This is to ensure unauthorised changes to data or information are prevented. So that such data or information can be trusted.

- **Availability:** This is to ensure that required data or information can be accessible at all time.

Security:

- **Online Security**: This is making use of technology to secure important information and data by implementing devices like firewall, access management software, use of protocols, use of encryption, etc.

- Physical Security: This is the securing of buildings or premises that business devices and data are kept. The location, the fencing, the use of CCTVs, the type of locks used, the use of security guards, the use of access technology, lighting effects, storage systems used, employing trust worthy and appropriate staff, physically securing laptops and desktops.

Risks: The possibility of damage happening and the ramifications of such damages, should they occur.

Threats: The potential to cause serious harm to a **computer** system. A **threat** is something that may or may not happen but has the potential to cause serious damage. **Threats** can lead to attacks on **computer** systems, networks and more. See below for examples:

- **Physical Threats:** Flood, Fire, War, Vandalism, Earthquake.

- **Accidental Errors:** Administrative, Programming or Software.

- **Unauthorised Access:** Information leakage, System hacking.

- **Malicious Misuse:** The corruption of software or information for fraudulent means.

- **Malware:** These are software programs designed to gain access to or damage computers or servers without the owner knowledge.

Attack: An attack is when an unauthorised person is able to access your system or data with or without your knowledge. Most attacks take place whenever a part or more of your system are vulnerable or not properly secure. Most attacks happen without your knowledge and by using sophisticated tools or applications which may cause harm to your system. A computer attack is any attempt to expose, alter, disable, destroy, steal or gain unauthorised access to or make unauthorised use of an asset.

A cyberattack is any type of offensive manoeuver employed by nation-states, individuals, group, society or organization that targets computer information systems, infrastructures, computer networks, and/or personal computer devices by various means of malicious acts usually originating from an anonymous source.

Hacker and Ethical Hacker:

- **Hacker:** Anyone with technical skills, often referring to a person who uses his or her abilities to gain unauthorized access to systems or networks in order to commit crimes.

- **Ethical Hacker:** A computer and networking expert who systematically attempts to penetrate a computer system or network on behalf of its owners for the purpose of finding security vulnerabilities that a malicious **hacker** could potentially exploit.

Attacks and counter measures:

- **Eavesdropping**, commonly known as 'message interception' is an attack on confidentiality by an unauthorised person. For example, wiretapping, message sniffing, and unauthorised copying of data. To prevent this from happening, make use of optic fibres for internet network instead of copper wires and use strong passwords to prevent people from gaining access to your system.

- **Tampering with Messages** is an attack on integrity, by stopping or delaying the flow of data in order to alter the information while in transit. To prevent this from happening, encrypt your information so that only the receiver is able to decrypt the message.

- **Fabrication of Messages** can be described as an attack on authenticity by masquerading as someone else and sending messages with this false identity. To prevent this from happening, ensure your personal details are not used when using unsecure systems and use strong encrypting methods when sending sensitive information, such as your date of birth and bank details.

- **Preventing Messages** is an attack on the availability of a service, or denial of it by causing the breakdown of the system or flooding the system with data, to make it impossible to maintain the processing speed. Sometimes it could be caused by an unauthorised person sending corrupted data into a system or physically damaging it. To prevent this from happening, adequate maintenance work should be done, allowing only vetted persons access to critical areas or systems and enhance security by installing CCTVs.

- **Virtualisation** is a form of technology which allows you to create images of actual or physical systems. For example; servers, storage device, network resources, desktop, hardware platforms, etc. This helps companies keep up with the pace of business growth by doubling the capacity and capability of physical systems. Other business benefits include time saving (during installations, software updates and maintenance), energy saving (reducing the number of active physical systems), minimising risks (getting systems back up and running after system failure or natural disaster and reduces data loss) and money saving.

- **Cloud Computing** is a method of using networked servers which are hosted on the internet to store, manage, and process data, in place of using remote servers or computers. In cloud computing, there are public and private service offers. A private cloud service supplier provides a dedicated cloud service to an individual or business customer, whereby all facilities such as infrastructure, storage, applications, etc. are used but not shared with any other cloud user. The Public or Multi-tenant cloud services, with the advent of virtualisation, are able to provide their facilities to multiple customers if and when required. For example, storage, applications, etc. are accessed over the internet by different organisations simultaneously. This is possible due to the method of virtualisation, where physical machines or infrastructure functionalities are duplicated using virtual machines (VMs).

- **Artificial Intelligence (AI)** are computer aided machines or tools capable of performing activities that are considered to be 'intelligent'. There are different categories of AI. They are the following; Applied is a system designed to deliver exceptional performance for a specific task. General is a system which performs the full range of intelligent (cognitive) task. Strong is the same system as the general but has its own consciousness and self-awareness. (Avira.com, 2018)

- **Zero-Day Threats** – These are new or unknown viruses or malware.

- **Cryptography** is the storing and transmitting of data according to a designed format, such that only those for whom it is intended have authorised access to it. Cryptography can be sub-divided into 'encryption' and 'decryption':

- **Encryption** is a method of hiding data either when in storage or being transmitted from unauthorised people. There are various methods which have been developed over the years.
- **Decryption** is a method used to reveal any hidden data or information. Only those authorised to see the data will be able to do so by using an agreed code to make it visible.

he way people store, or send important or private data today has changed onsiderably when compared to methods used in the past. Reason being, mprovement in technology has given businesses or individuals better and asier ways to keep their data secure. However, on the other hand the mprovement in technology and the high percentage use of the internet, have lso armed hackers with weapons of destruction. Hackers are able to identify ulnerable systems, i.e. those deemed inadequate or lacking security, and ccess such systems to help themselves to business data or private nformation. Most organisations are fighting back by improving their security ystems and also changing their security strategies to prevent hackers from enetrating their systems or reducing the impact of unauthorised access or acking.

yber Security has improved the awareness globally around information and ata security. Depending on the size of the organisation, the structure of the T department could include Cyber Security experts or be separated as security epartment. As a separate department, the security staff will work with all the ther departments to drive the organisational security policy in line with usiness objectives. The role of the information security department will be to:

- Improve security awareness within the organisation.

- To identify potential threats.

- Carry out risk analysis using available methods.

- Ensure the required solutions are put in place.

It is part of their duties to decide whether it would be reasonable to employ an **ethical hacker** to constantly check for system vulnerabilities within the organisations network or devices, to advice senior management and customers of the method of **encryption and decryption** that will be used to keep stored or transit data secure. They will be in a good position to advise the organisation on the simple mistakes that staff make like opening of virus infected emails. They will also work with senior management to decide when to carry out regular **internal audits** and **penetration** (intrusive) **testing**, so as to maintain a healthy and secure network and systems. The security department will also be available to provide required information during a visit by **external auditors**.

It is a known practice for the information security or Cyber Security department to employ people from various professions to work as security staff. For example, lawyers, engineers, network administrators, project managers, testers, etc. This gives them a wide range of field experience that will help deal with security decisions and improve on solutions needed to keep their systems, data and environment secure.

CHAPTER 2: Information Security Standards & Common Threats

There are two main organisations responsible for setting security standards. They are the 'International Organisation for Standardisation' (ISO) and the 'International Electro-technical commission' (IEC). This is a global joint technical committee that ensures security practices and technology used, adhere to agreed security standards. There are a series of rules and regulations which govern proceedings. These rules and regulations (or standards) were developed and maintained by ISO/IEC. Hence, every organisation has to show that they are compliant with these standards, otherwise, they will be penalised which could be a financial burden. An example of said standards is the ISO/IEC 27000, which represents a family of information security management system standards.

Common Security Threats

These are threats which have made their rounds globally and are still happening in most computer systems today. This is not an exhaustive list but gives you an idea of the types of known threats affecting businesses and individuals.

- **Computer virus'** are programs which can duplicate itself and infect computers or servers without the knowledge of the owner. Virus' can only spread from one computer to another. Once data or files in a computer are infected by virus' and the file or data is sent to another computer, the receiving computer is infected as well when the information is accessed. The spread of computer virus' are enhanced once a computer is linked to the internet.

- **Computer worms** are self-replicating computer programs, which rely on the computer network to transmit copies of itself to another linked computer and computer network. They are different from viruses because they do not require a carrier or files on which to be attached in order to spread.

- **Trojan**, commonly known as, "Trojan horses" are computer programs which are designed to perform malicious functions on the target machines or systems such as providing unauthorised access to the target machines. They will also enable the intruders to gain entry every so often into the target machines without suspicion.

- **Spyware** are computer programs which are installed on the target computers to monitor the user's interactions, activities and websites visited. They can also secretly steal personal information, change computer settings and could redirect website browser activities.

- **Phishing** is a process of fraudulently obtaining sensitive or personal information from a target computer or system by masquerading as a trusted user.

- **E-mail Spam** or "junk emails" are a combination of unsolicited messages or viral infected and/or malicious contents, that are sent to a large number of email addresses.

- **Scareware** are fake products which are sold to victims to remedy a fictitious computer problem that the product was responsible for creating initially. In turn, this means that the victim is at the mercy of the criminal to help solve an unknown problem.

- **Hackers** use various tools, techniques and strategies in order to gain access to their victim's information. As opportunists, they tend to strike when the necessary precautions are not implemented.

- **Pharming** is an example of online fraud, where a genuine web address is re-directed to a malicious website. The illegitimate website is spoofed to look the same as a legitimate website and it is often difficult to differentiate between the two.

- **Ransomware** is a type of malware which prevents the victim accessing their computer or data. The victim is presented with a message demanding a ransom before access can be re-established.

- **WIFI eavesdropping** is when an unauthorised person uses a tool to listen in on communication both over a virtual and unsecure network without the legitimate users' knowledge. Personal and private information, such as credit card details and passwords are easily obtained.

- **Mobile phones/iPad attacks** are attacks which happen due to the increased popularity of online banking. Mobile phones are infected by programs designed by criminals to retrieve login details of the victim, in order to gain access to bank accounts. Mobile phone owners are vulnerable whenever they are sending data or money over unsecure networks because their information and money is at risk of being hijacked.

- **Attacks** on **small and medium sized businesses**, can be a result of complacency whereby SMBs think they do not have anything of value when compared to large or blue chip companies. However, since they hold personal information in the form of customer data, criminals could easily steal this, which could then be profitable.

- **Uneducated users** refers to those computer users who have a limited understanding of the level of risks associated with connecting their devices to the internet. Without basic training and constantly updating their knowledge on daily cyber threats they are likely to be easily impacted. For example, clicking on an infected email.

- **User errors** are made by those who lack awareness of Cyber Security or behave carelessly. For example, sending private or sensitive data over an unsecure network or without encrypting their data when in transit.

HAPTER 3: Protecting your systems and network

here are important actions which should be taken to protect your systems ndividually or as a business. Consider actions like installing software at trategic points of the business network and on individual computers to serve s a gate keeper against incoming data. These installed gate keepers cannot uarantee stopping all infected data from getting through your network and our computer.

ome software is installed to continually monitor the internal parts and files of our computer for infected data which has passed through the gate keeper's efences. These software are known as **antivirus** software. There are well-nown types of antivirus software, which are used to identify, isolate and liminate the majority of the threats mentioned in the section above, before hey cause irreparable damage, to your system. To ensure these threats are ot missed, the antivirus will remain active by running at intervals in any active ystem. They are easy to install and updating the software is done utomatically via an online process, whenever there is something new to add o the older version. Antivirus softwares check aspects such as; emails, nachine compatibility, phone compatibility, operating system, firewall, etc. Aost of them produce statistical information after every run, to enable the ser to understand the level of work the software has done on your system nd will also highlight any major threats encountered and eliminated.

ntivirus software are developed by different manufacturers and their level of erformance vary depending on their suitability to the platforms or systems hey are applied to. For the majority of them, you have to pay for the license efore you can make use of them. It is advised to renew your license annually. he producers can also develop bespoke copies for a company's on request, nd this would invariably perform better to suit their system at a reasonable ost overall. However, it should be noted that there are some free antivirus oftware programs as well. Free antivirus software can be downloaded directly nline.

It is good practice, before purchasing any antivirus software, to read the reviews on them from existing users or to ask any reputable software house to recommend an appropriate one for your system.

Internet Safety and Social Media

Internet users must always think of safety whenever or wherever they are using the internet. Over the years on social media, we have heard things like bullying, sexting, stress, suicide, use of abusive language, addiction, etc. To ensure we continue to enjoy the positive aspects of the internet, we must practice the things we do well offline, when we are online. For example, bullying in real life situations is unlawful. Therefore, cyber bullying should be treated the same. Any inappropriate language or behaviour noticed online should be reported to the authority in charge of that platform as soon as possible, and where appropriate it should be reported to the police as well. There are some social media platforms which do not permit children of certain age groups to register as members. In light of this, it would not be fitting for an adult or parent to register as a member and allow their under age children access to those sites. Combining well-mannered and apt behaviour online, with the guidance of industry professionals, the internet will always be a window of opportunities that will serve us well.

CHAPTER 4: Artificial Intelligence (AI) and Cyber Security

Artificial Intelligence has been a prominent advancement in the field of technology. However, AI often meets a degree of negativity, due to having inadequate ethical justifications when making certain decisions. For example, it is not possible to teach a machine to overcome gender and racial biases. There are no legal frameworks in place to deal with system errors where complete control is given to AI. Where large volumes of data are analysed, data privacy becomes a key concern and even with all the technological advancement, human intervention is necessary. There is a general consensus that as long as humans remain in control and follow the required guidelines, AI and machine learning will benefit humanity.

It should be noted that Cyber Security solutions currently are protective, reactive and able to eliminate identified or known threats, but still struggle with preventing Zero-Day or evolving threats. AI and machine learning can make a big difference in this area. Research has shown on some systems where AI solutions were applied successfully, that threats prevention is at a very high level.

The following benefits were achieved; the replacement of ineffective antivirus software and intrusion detection tools, prediction of future or evolving threats, reduce cost of mitigation and remediation of compromised systems. (2017, Cylance eBook).

CHAPTER 5: Cyber Essentials and Essential Plus

In order to help UK businesses, prevent the barrages of cyber-attacks, the National Cyber Security Council has developed a couple of programmes called "Cyber Essentials" and "Essentials Plus". The national council approves nominated companies as an "Accrediting Body" and these companies, in alignment with the national council authority provide the processes and guidelines for training and examining interested companies to become a "Certification Body". These certifying institutions' duties include supporting all types of businesses to ensure they remain compliant with the cyber essentials requirements by carrying out audits, testing and regular systems reviews. Naturally, as the contents of cyber essentials become enhanced or evolve, these changes will reflect throughout the Accrediting and Certification Bodies processes. The "Cyber Essential Plus" is the advance certification of the cyber essentials programme. These programmes will enable most businesses to remain proactive in the combat of future cyber threats.

For someone to become Cyber Essentials certified, they need to pay for a couple of days training with any of the certifying bodies. A candidate is required to have some level of computer systems and network knowledge before attending the training. At the end of the training, a candidate is required to pass a written exam before the certificate is issued. With this certificate, a candidate is qualified to support businesses to identify security gaps to ensure they are compliant with Cyber Essentials requirements.

Cyber Essential Plus (which is a more advanced training) is a separate course from Cyber Essentials. Which means a candidate has to successfully complete Cyber Essential course as prerequisite before attending the Essential Plus course.

CHAPTER 6: General Data Protection Regulation (GDPR)

From the 25th May 2018, General Data Protection Regulation, i.e. GDPR, became effective as a component of European law. GDRP came into play in order to protect individuals personal data, stored in business databases. It gives authority to the data owner and allows them to control how their data is being used, as well as having the power to remove their data from any given database. Hence, as of the 25th of May 2018, every institution must seek authorisation from their customers to keep their data and also inform their customers how they intend to use their data going forward. The customer can at any time withdraw their consent, whereby the institution must then stop using the customer's data or remove it completely from their system. Wherever third-party businesses are involved in the use of the customers' data, institutions or businesses must inform their customers about it. Consequently, in the event of a breach of this regulation, a heavy fine will be imposed depending on the severity of the offence. Institutions are compelled to inform the regulator within 72 hours of their systems being compromised. In other words, whenever an institution or business system is hacked, they have 72 hours from the time they notice the hacking had taken place to make it public. Failure to comply with this law, means an offender could face a penalty of 4% of their GDP or 17 million pounds (which ever one is greater).

CHAPTER 7: Education and Certification

Due to the importance of cyber or information security in our society at large, there are various courses being run in most institutions today and early introductory courses are also now available in some Universities at undergraduate level. However, higher level and advanced courses are provided by Universities at a Master's level. To ensure a Master's degree offers the level of competence needed by organisations and businesses to deal with the issues facing cyber or information security, the courses offered in UK institutions, have been tailored to align with the **Government Communications Headquarters (GCHQ)** guidelines. Universities are expected to apply to GCHQ for accreditation as indication that they'll abide by GCHQ's guidelines. Some private institutions also provide courses like data analyst, security administrator, penetration testing etc. With this training, people are able to work in information security environments or businesses.

Aside from the degree programmes, Cyber Security professionals can also obtain certification to show their level of knowledge, either as experts such as consultants, or to specialise in a particular area of Cyber Security. The certifications include;

- **Certified Information Systems Professional (CISSP)** – Leadership and Operations: **CISSP** is an information security certification developed by the International Information Systems Security Certification Consortium, also known as $(ISC)^2$.

- **Systems Security Certified Practitioner (SSCP) – IT Administration** - The $(ISC)^2$ is an entry-level information security certification, and it is the ideal precursor for the much sought-after Certified Information Systems Security Professional (CISSP).

- **Cisco Certified Security Professional (CCSP)** – Cloud Security is an IT (Information Technology) professional who has received formal training from Cisco Systems in network-related security hardware, software and management. CCSPs are employed in IT security departments and as system administrators.

- **Certified Authorization Professional (CAP)** is a vendor-neutral individual with skills and experience in implementing and maintaining authorisation on Information Systems.

- **Certified Secure Software Lifecycle Professional (CSSLP)** is a certification which shows knowledge and understanding of Software development security.

- **HealthCare Information Security and Privacy Practitioner (HCISPP)** is a certification which shows knowledge in managing or the processing of security patient information in healthcare.

- **Certified Information Systems Auditor (CISA)** is a certification issued by ISACA for the people in charge of ensuring that an organization's IT and business systems are monitored, managed and protected. It is designed for IT auditors, audit managers, consultants and security professionals.

CHAPTER 8: Roles & Responsibilities in Cyber Security

The organisational structure, company size and business objectives will determine the required roles that will be created within a corporation. These roles should be clearly defined in terms of their functions and level of responsibilities within the organisation.

The key roles in the area of information or Cyber Security are the following;

- **A Chief Information Officer (CIO)** is responsible for the strategic use and management of information systems and technology within an organisation. A CIO shares working time dealing with technology related queries and business-related queries. This role will normally report to the Chief Executive Officer (CEO) or Chief Financial Officer (CFO) of the organisation. Due to their responsibilities, a CIO will work closely with the CEO and other members of senior management. The role is also responsible for the organisation's security program and the protection of all organisational assets.

- **A Chief Privacy Officer (CPO)** is necessary due to the requirements for organisations to secure all types of data, such as customer, company, and staff. This ensures organisations are protected from law suits, if there are any breaches. Due to this legal factor, this role will be better suited for a legal practitioner and as such a CPO will be responsible for developing the organisation's policies, standards, procedures, controls and contract agreements to ensure privacy requirements are being met.

- **Chief Information Security Officer's(CISO)** are employed within most organisation, whether large, medium or small sized, and are responsible for answering security queries which are passed to the IT department to handle. This role will ensure security requirements and business needs amalgamate together. A CISO is responsible for assessing the organisational risks and solutions in order to mitigate those risks. This role will also play a part in the creation and maintenance of security programs which will improve the organisation's business drivers. Furthermore, a CISO will handle organisational compliance of legal and IT regulations, including customer's expectations and contractual obligations.

- **IT Security Consultants (SC)** are required to commensurate with cyber-security, risk management, compliance auditing, testing, customer service and information assurance. A security consultant is the key point of contact for most security issues. Security consultants can have a range of different job titles, such as information security consultant, computer security consultant, cyber-security consultant, database security consultant, compliance security consultant, network security consultant and private sector security consultant.

- **A Security Architect (SA)** is responsible for planning, analysing, designing, testing, maintaining and supporting an enterprise's critical infrastructure.

- **A Security Engineer (SE protects** company assets from threats, with a focus on quality control within the IT infrastructure.

The positions above cover specialist areas, which are relevant to the respective job titles. However, at its core, an IT security consultant is required to be well versed in cyber-security, risk management, compliance auditing, testing, customer service, and information assurance. An IT security consultant is the key point of contact for all these areas.

As a professional in this field you must be able to keep up to date with the fast-moving IT landscape and possess a range of superior IT skills. You must be able to communicate effective strategies with a range of stakeholders. As a consultant, you will be expected to identify gaps in current IT practices and recommend best practice solutions to reduce risk and maximise business opportunities.

The following roles are also important in the field of Cyber Security. However, some of them may reside in a separate department but will continue to work closely with security professionals when dealing with security issues:

- **Data owner or Information Owners** are at a management level and are responsible for the protection and use of specific information, in the event of any negligent act that results in the corruption or disclosure of data. He/ she decides upon the classification of data they are responsible for and data editing when necessary, ensuring that security controls are in place. He/she will define security requirements per classification and backup requirements, approving any disclosure activities, ensuring that proper access rights are being used. Data owner or information owner usually defines user access activities and approves access requests (although they may choose to delegate this function). Responsibilities also include dealing with security violation pertaining to the data they are responsible for and delegating the day to day maintenance of the data protection mechanism to the data custodian.

- **A GDPR Data Protection Officer** is responsible for an organisation's data processing activities and in charge of data protection impact assessment. The Data Protection Officer is also the point of contact on issues regarding GDPR.

- **A Data custodian** is responsible for maintaining and protecting data. The role requires IT or security experience. Duties include implementing and maintaining security controls, performing regular backups of the data, periodically validating the integrity of the data, restoring data from backup media, retaining records of activity, and fulfilling the requirements specified in the company's security policy, standards and guidelines that pertain to information security and data protection.

- **System Owners** look after one or more systems, each of which may hold and process data owned by different data owners. Responsibilities include integrating security considerations into application and system purchasing decisions and development projects. The system owner is responsible for ensuring that adequate security is being provided by the necessary controls, password management, remote access controls, operating system configurations, etc. This role must ensure the systems are properly assessed for vulnerabilities and must report any to the incident response team and data owner.

- **Penetration Tester or Pen Tester**s practice the testing of a computer system, network or web application to find vulnerabilities that an attacker could exploit. A Pen tester carries out a combination of intrusive and non-intrusive systems' tests.

- An **Ethical hacker** is a computer and networking expert who systematically attempts to penetrate a computer system or network on behalf of its owners for the purpose of finding security vulnerabilities that a malicious hacker could potentially exploit.

- **Security administrators** are responsible for implementing and maintaining specific security network devices and software in the enterprise. These controls include firewalls, IDS, IPS, antimalware, security proxies, data loss prevention, etc. The main focus here is to keep the network secure.

- A **Security analyst** works at a higher, more strategic level than the aforementioned job roles and helps develop policies, standards, and guidelines, as well as set various baselines. This role helps define the security program elements and follows through to ensure the elements are being carried out and practiced properly. A Security Analyst tends to work at a design level than at the implementation level.

- **Data analysts** are responsible for ensuring that data is stored in a way that makes the most sense both for the company and the individuals who need to access and work with it. For example, payroll information should not be mixed with inventory information. The purchasing department needs to have a lot of its values in monetary terms, and the inventory system must follow a standardized naming scheme. Working closely alongside the data owner, a data analyst helps ensure that the structures set up coincide with and support the company's business objectives.

- **Auditor** are responsible for periodical visits to company's, ensuring business' are doing what they are supposed to be doing. They ensure the correct controls are in place and are being maintained securely. This role's goal is to ensure the organisation complies with its own policies and the applicable laws and regulations. Organisations can have internal and external auditors. The external auditors commonly work on behalf of a regulatory body to make sure compliance is being met.

CHAPTER 9: Starting a career in Cyber Security

1. **Keep up to date with the field of Cyber Security.**

It is beneficial to find out information about the activities and issues covered in Cyber Security, by reading books on fundamentals of Cyber Security and proactively browsing the internet. If you work for an organisation where Cyber Security is practiced, it would advantageous to obtain in-house documents to source valuable knowledge.

2. **Frequently liaise with industry professionals.**

Delving into the field of Cyber Security can be a daunting one for a layman who has minimal experience. Always try to fill in the gaps in the information you have gathered, by speaking to industry professionals. By gauging their experience, responsibilities and career journey, you will be able to ascertain the appropriate decisions to take in forming your own career. By building on these valuable relationships, it might well be that you can gain work experience under the aforementioned industry professionals.

3. **Consider the existing transferable skills you possess, that can be implemented in the field of Cyber Security.**

Consider where your current skills could be of benefit in the field of Cyber security. If you are already working in an organisation which operates a Cyber Security department, start to think or enquire about the possibility of providing support in the Cyber Security department based on your own personal skill set. However, if you are not working in an IT related business then speak to a security professional to ascertain whether your skill set will be a valuable contribution within a Cyber Security environment. This is important because there might be a vacancy which requires your current skills with a caveat to provide you with the security training. Having IT or technical skills will be handy but is not mandatory.

4. **Organise a face to face meeting with recruitment agencies.**

Approach and arrange meetings with recruitment agencies which specialise in Cyber Security. This is important because they are able to update you with current market trends in this field. They will be in a position to say what employers are looking for in a potential employee. As specialists in Cyber Security recruitment, these experts will be able to elaborate on the kinds of training and certification required based on individual's skills. They are in a better position to confirm the pay scale for the security roles too.

5. **Consider a couple of roles and responsibilities of interest in Cyber security.**

Consider the Cyber Security roles and responsibilities which stands out for you. These are the roles you are happy to do if and when you have the required skills. For example, Data Analyst and GDPR Protection security Officer roles.

6. **Research into the requirements for each of the roles selected in no 5 above.**

For those roles, what are the required skills to do the jobs? What do you require in terms of training to enable you fill in any skill gaps identified? From your current position, how long will it take to update the skills' shortage and become ready to apply for a job? Would it be possible to complete training in a shorter time, if the training is acquired via the apprenticeship route or a job shadow or work experience? Providing answers to these questions would determine the best way forward.

7. **Arrange the necessary training in order to develop relevant new skills.**

Depending on your skills shortage, this should determine the type of training to go for. There are Cyber Security companies which provide free security training but most of them come with specific criteria attached to it. For example, free training might be provided for people within a particular catchment area or employment status. Search and arrange the appropriate course or training. Ensure that the training is provided by a reputable organisation, to ensure that the certificate issued after the training is accepted by employers. This could be confirmed by an esteemed recruitment agency. Most security training is completed by sitting a written exam at the end of the training and a certificate is issued if successful.

8. **Register with professional organisations and attend events or conferences.**

Register with IT and security professional bodies, such as the British Computer Society (BCS) and the Institute of Information security Professionals (IISP). As someone who is interested in Cyber security, it is a good practice to attend security events and conferences regularly. This provides you with networking opportunities and updates in terms of how the security industry is changing. By doing this, you'll be able to appreciate efforts made by the Cyber Security community in relation to working together to deal with key issues and you will be exposed to newly developed security tools as they come into the market.

See Appendix B in chapter 10 for a step by step flowchart.

CHAPTER 10: Summary

Cyber Security is a field that is forever growing. New threats can be discovered on a daily basis in your organisation or business. New technologies are developed all the time to counter the threats, etc. In turn, you have to constantly keep updating your knowledge and skills to enable you to deal with the ever-present threats. In this field, team work or sharing ideas to develop counter measures are very important in ensuring most threats are mitigated or prevented from happening.

The internet has changed the way we do things for the better. However, it is important to continue to communicate, collaborate, share our experiences with one another and apply common sense where necessary to ensure online safety.

During the period of using AI as an alternative security solution, it became apparent that harnessing the predictive and protective capabilities of AI and machine learning reduces the quantity of other security solutions that are required. This will inevitably boost the efficiency of systems and increase the rate at which attacks are prevented. With the rise in daily threats to businesses and individual systems, formidable threat busting solutions will be produced, by combining human intelligence, effective security tools and AI (enhanced by machine learning) capabilities.

With GDPR in operation, it would be beneficial for every EU resident to review their business dealings with most institutions, including those you haven't communicated with for a long time. For businesses to be GDPR compliant, they must request consent from the customer before making use of their data. They should consider employing the services of a data protection officer, who will be responsible for carrying out the data protection impact assessment. Whenever there is a data breach, the business must report the incident within 72 hours to the authorities.

You do not need to be a degree holder or have technical experience in IT to work in the field of Cyber Security. However, there are some roles which are mandated to be held by people with a degree and a number of years of commercial experience. The certification requirements vary as you go from one organisation to another but in general, being certified gives an individual a better chance of employment or to getting their contract approved.

The field of Cyber Security is made up of people from different professional backgrounds. So, each profession brings their knowledge and work experience together with others to ensure confidentiality, integrity and availability of information or data are maintained, which are the key components of Cyber Security.

Cyber Security will ensure that authorised users gain access to information without problems and prevent unauthorised access or hacking of any system. Access of a system will often be explained using the basic components of confidentiality, integrity and availability as defined above.

It must be noted that even with all the security techniques, standards, and technology, there is no system or environment that is 100% secure. What is paramount to an organisation, is preventing and minimising the impact on their business, whenever their system or data is breached or compromised.

Other useful information -

or additional information, please visit the following websites;

- The Government Communication Headquarters (GCHQ) **: The official website**
- National Cyber Security Centre (NCSC) **: The official website**

References –

- **Tech Targets,** https://searchsoftwarequality.techtarget.com
- **ISO,** https://www.iso.org/home.html
- **IEC,** http://www.iec.ch/
- https://www.itgovernance.co.uk/what-is-cybersecurity
- https://safeandsecureonline.org/
- https://www.cylance.com
- https://www.avira.com

Appendix A: Relationships in the field of Cyber Security

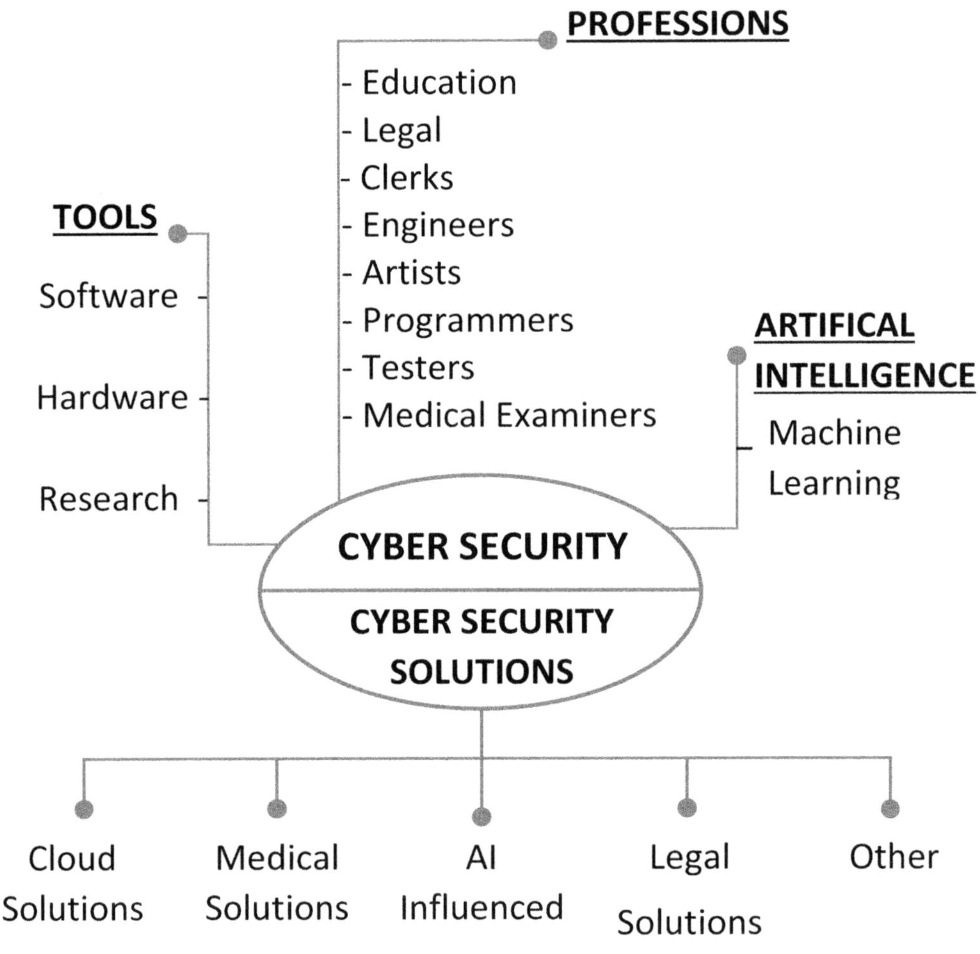

Appendix B: Starting a career in Cyber security flowchart

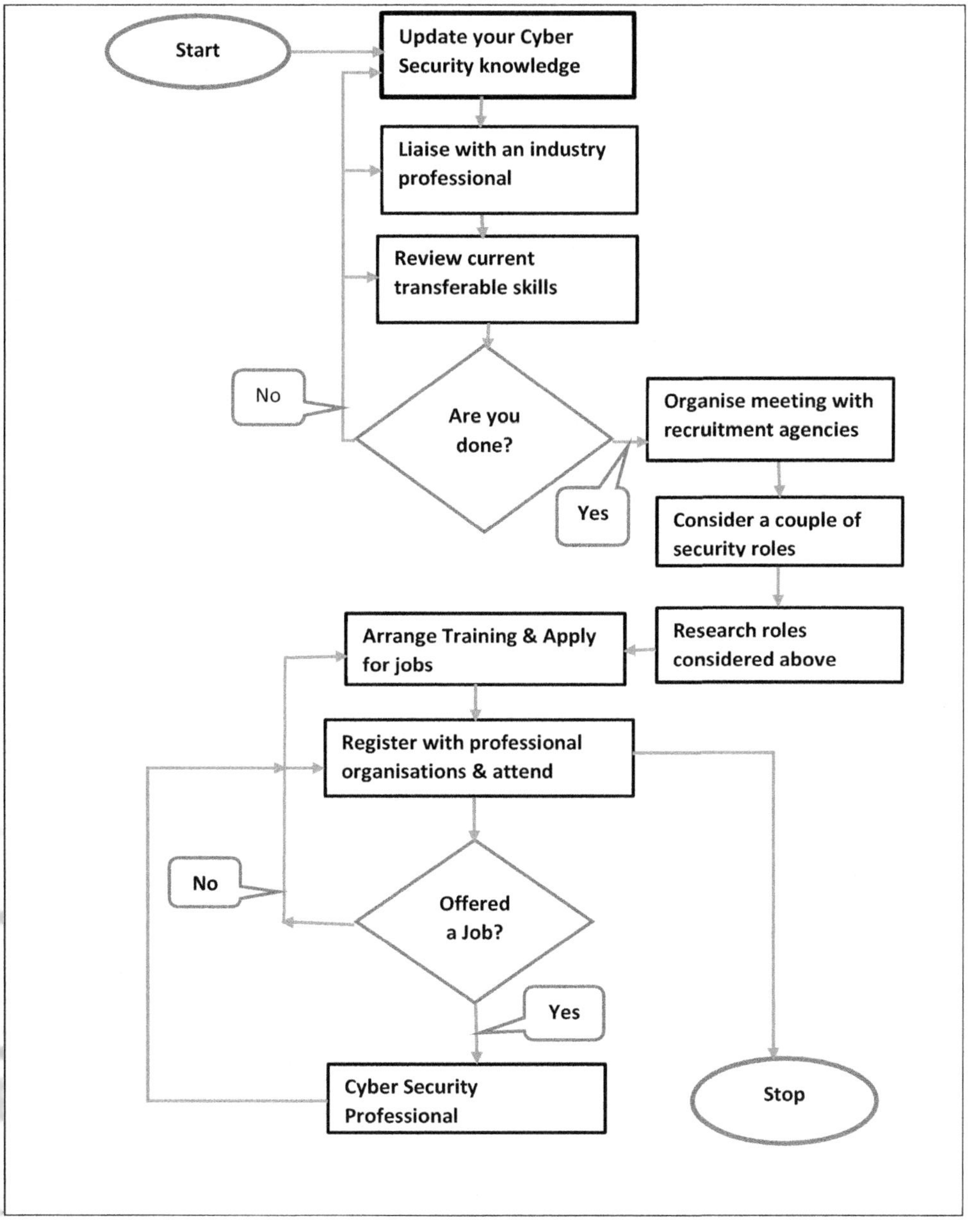

Printed in Great Britain
by Amazon

80520379R00031